James Taylor

Everyday Parables

Learnings from Life

To Mel
as food for
thought.

Jim Taylor

WOOD LAKE BOOKS

Editor: Michael Schwartzentruber
Cover design: Lois Huey Heck
Photos: Jim Taylor, Michael Schwartzentruber

Canadian Cataloguing in Publication Data

Taylor, James, 1936–
    Everyday Parables

ISBN 1–55154–055–0
1. Christian life–Meditations. I. Title.
BV4832.2.T387 1995   248   C95–910709–6

Printing 10 9 8 7 6 5 4 3 2

Published by
Wood Lake Books Inc.
10162 Newene Road
Winfield, BC Canada V4V 1R2

Printed in Canada by
Hignell Printing Ltd.
Winnipeg, MB, R3G 2B4

Dedication

To all the people in all the groups who have tried creating their own everyday parables, and discovered how exciting the process can be. Almost all of the parables in this book originated with one or more of those groups. I assigned the topics; they provided the insights. I couldn't give due credit to each of the groups, partly because I have notes of the insights, but usually not of the sources, and partly because several groups may have provided insights on the same topic.

Contents

Introduction ✦ 7

Introduction

In one sense, this book is a beginner's guide to theological reflection. And so I've made it deliberately lightweight. It's 128 pages of starter kit. It's a set of booster cables. It's "Coles' Notes" on theological reflection on everyday life.

I believe that the vast majority of Christians today have given up expecting to discern God most of the time.

It's no coincidence, I'm convinced, that younger people attend church less regularly than older ones. According to University of Lethbridge sociologist Reginald Bibby, some 37% of people aged 55 and over attend church weekly; that figure drops to 23% for people aged 35–54, and to only 14% for those between the ages of 18–34. Many hypotheses have been offered for this slide, most of them based on social demographics or pop psychology.

I'm surprised that an obvious correlation has been so commonly overlooked – the more technologically complex the world into which people were born, the less likely they are to go to church.

As I write this, my father is 90 years old. When he was born, in 1905, most people in rural Ontario still traveled by horse and cart. Cars had been invented, but were still rare.

A few years ago, some friends and I sat at a table at Tim Faller's wedding reception. His great-grandmother sat across the table from us. She was 99 years old at the time. She'd been born a decade before the turn of the century. In her lifetime, she has seen the advent of air flight, of cars, of telephones, of recorded music, of radio and television, of transistors and computers, of electricity, of petroleum fuels... The world she was born into knew nothing of ozone depletion or acid rain or global warming. It had never been threatened by nuclear warfare. The forests and the fish were thought inexhaustible.

The first time we took our daughter Sharon to Ireland, she looked out the car window one dreary day when the rain sluiced horizontally across emerald green fields, and asked, "Dad, what are those fuzzy-looking rocks out there?"

Just then one of the "rocks" got up and shook itself.

"They're sheep," I explained.

She went into paroxysms of laughter. I never did find out what she expected sheep to look like, but it certainly wasn't fuzzy rocks.

In that brief exchange, though, I realized how meaningless a central image of the Bible must be to her. If she didn't know anything at all about sheep, how was she to understand Jesus' parables about sheep? How could she comprehend, "The Lord is my shepherd..."?

There has been more change in this century than in all the other 19 centuries since the time of Jesus. At the turn of the last century, people still lived pretty much as biblical people did. They might have worked in heavy industry, but in their homes they still used lamps and hand tools that people from biblical times could recognize.

But what would biblical people make of a modern dishwasher? Or a microwave oven? Or a stereo set playing compact discs of a full orchestra and chorus?

At 58, I can still remember enough of a former world that the stories of the Bible mean something to me. But how much can a teenager born into the computer age, a young adult born since the Vietnam war, a child who has never known a time when people did not have satellites hovering in the sky – how much can these newcomers have in common with a community of people who express their faith mostly in meaningless images of a long-ago time?

The problem is not that the story of God, the message of Jesus, is out of date. The problem is that we Christians have been content to express it in outdated images and metaphors. We've been content to let someone else – a few years or a few centuries ago – do our theological reflection for us.

During the last year, I've been having correspondence (written and electronic) with a variety of people about a faith suited to the new millennium that is rushing towards us. Initially, we had a great deal of difficulty trying to agree on any kind of definition of how we understood God. Then someone pointed out that we reveal the kind of God we believe in much more in the stories we tell than in the definitions we develop.

As a community of faith, the stories we tell reveal that God is not present in this world. God was present in biblical times. God may have been present during the medieval period, and during the Reformation. God may be known in the German theological colleges of the early part of this century, or in the *barrios* and *favelas* of Latin America, or in the unspoiled wilderness of a national park. But God is not here in our four-wheel drive minivans, or our 28,800 baud modems, or our computer-generated pension cheques.

Because we simply do not talk about God when we talk about those things. Whatever our doctrines affirm, our stories reveal that God is irrelevant to 90% of our lives.

And so, over the last few years, I have led workshops in which I asked people to create their own parables around everyday things.

They've had a lot of fun and I've learned a lot from their insights. For example, in my book *Two Worlds in One* (Wood Lake Books, 1985), I tell about a particular group of men; I asked this group to "Consider the pine cone..."

They came up with some surprising conclusions.

The pine cone's mission, they decided, is to carry seeds, to grow new pine trees. Like a pine cone, our mission is to plant seeds of faith in new people.

There are more seeds than can ever turn into pine trees – like the abundance of God's grace.

But a pine cone can't plant its seeds without opening up. In the same way, we can't spread the good news if we remain closed, sealed up, protecting our faith from a hostile world around us.

Then a man from another group, who'd been listening, stood up excitedly... The trees outside our room, he explained, were lodgepole pines. Some of their cones will only open under intense heat. Summer sunlight simply isn't strong enough. Only a forest fire has enough heat to make those cones open. As it destroys other trees, the fire opens the lodgepole pine's cones, and seeds a new forest.

In that way, an agent of destruction becomes a means of salvation, of re-creation.

"It's kind of like the crucifixion and the resurrection," said the man, struggling to explain his insight. "Maybe those cones are telling us that before something new can be born, something old has to die."

I think Jesus would have liked that parable.

Do you see how these parables work? You take some familiar object, something you've never thought of as having any religious significance, and analyze it. What's it made of? What's it used for? How does it work? You list those qualities, without worrying about how important they are, or whether they're "religious" qualities.

Then you compare that list with your faith. Or with God. Or with the church. Or the Bible...

And suddenly you're making connections that you never thought were there.

It is in this sense, then, that this book is a "beginner's guide." If we are to start telling stories that include God in our daily world, we have to start with the apparently insignificant stuff. The local stuff. The everyday stuff that's so common we habitually overlook it. There is no point in practicing theological reflection about international politics when we can't do theological reflection about peeling potatoes.

Things really matter only when they come close to home. I've watched church assemblies vote unanimously for resolutions that instruct national governments to change their monetary policies or to get rid of racial discrimination. The heated debate comes over whether clergy need to declare their honoraria for weddings and funerals on their income tax, and whether congregations can be required to accept a gay minister.

Jesus did not build his parables on what one head of state said to another head of state. He talked about ordinary, everyday things. In them, he found evidence of the nature and purpose of God.

So must we.

You may look at these pages and say, "What? A potato peeler? A door hinge? A pair of shoelaces? What's religious about those things?" And you may remember that there's nothing particularly religious about sheep, or vines, or salt, either. We only give them significance when we associate them with religious truths.

In the same way, we will give significance to every aspect of our lives when we can associate those things with what we know of God and the church, of Jesus and our faith.

And that really *will* be profound.

Use it or lose it

Imagine that someone asked you, "What is God trying to tell you right now?" while you were doing the laundry, or nailing siding onto your house...

If you're quick witted and memorized a lot of Bible verses as a child, you might come up with word associatons about washing away sin, or building houses on a rock.

But until you were asked, it wouldn't have occurred to you that what you were doing had any connection with your faith! And if you were asked the same questions when you were working on the car, or boarding a jumbo jet, you couldn't have answered at all. Because automatic transmissions and airlines aren't mentioned in the Bible...

By and large, our churches today have lost the message of Emmanuel, the name that means "God with us." The preaching, the teaching, the thinking almost always focus on long, long ago. People have given up expecting to find God anywhere other than in church or in the Bible.

That puts their faith into a strait jacket.

– from An Everyday God, *(Wood Lake Books, 1981), p. 9*

◆   ◆   ◆

A fairly high proportion of the parables created by groups focus on their Christian faith. Not on any particular aspect of their faith. Not on any specific doctrine. But simply on having faith at all. It's as if the parable-makers feel themselves at odds with their friends and community, a bit like aliens in a foreign land.

One person said, after a parables session, "At last I'm able to talk to people about my faith in ways that make sense to them."

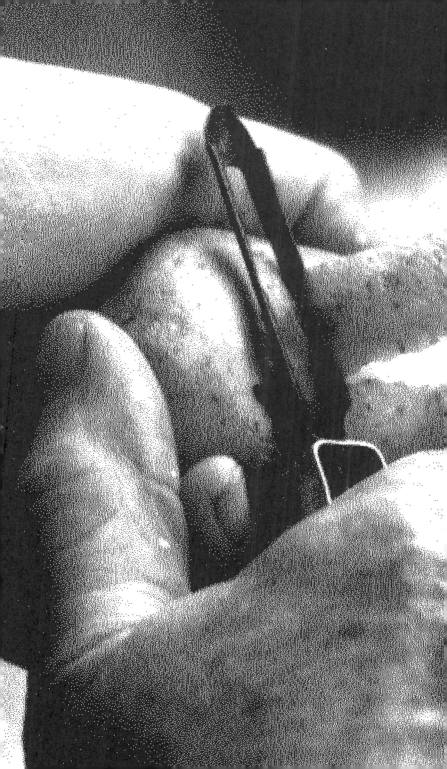

Potato peeler

It was, I think, the first time I had ever risked asking people to try creating their own parables.

They were a group of women, in Beamsville, at the west end of Lake Ontario. I wanted to have them think of something they all knew well, but had never thought of as having any religious significance.

A potato peeler.

It cuts away the skin, they noted. It gets rid of the unsightly and dirty part of a potato, so that one can get at the good stuff within. A religious perspective may help us do the same for the less pleasant parts of our culture – it enables us to cut through the crud, and see what's really worthwhile, the good stuff of modern life.

A good potato peeler wastes as little as possible – so should our faith.

"And have you noticed?" one woman asked the others. "You can't protect a potato peeler by keeping it tucked away in a drawer. A potato peeler is kept sharp by constant use..."

She didn't have to finish the point.

Hatchet

My father gave me a hatchet when I was 12. A hatchet might seem like a dangerous gift to give a child. Perhaps it was. But I learned to use it safely. I learned how to hit the mark with it. Not a bit to this side, nor a bit to that side, but exactly where I wanted that blade to penetrate.

I learned to keep it sharp. A dull hatchet, I discovered, is much more dangerous than a sharp one. A sharp hatchet, with the edge properly filed, bites deep into the wood; a dull hatchet glances off and buries itself in your shin.

In later years, I heard educators arguing about whether children could, or should, be taught the Bible. The Bible is too complex a book, some of them said. If adults have trouble dealing with it, how can we expect children to? Its message requires a level of understanding that children haven't reached yet...

I think the Bible may be like my hatchet.

You have to start somewhere. Neither skill nor safety arrives automatically at a certain age – an axe, in the hands of an unskilled adult, is just as hazardous as a hatchet in the hands of a child. I was so small, I swung that puny hatchet two-handed. But I did learn how to swing it.

A dull mind is as dangerous as a dull hatchet – it too is likely to glance off its intended target and do damage somewhere else.

And you have to keep in practice. I can swing a full size axe now. But I can't split a matchstick any more, because I haven't been practicing my skills. Hopefully, I've done better with my faith.

Music

Have you ever noticed – there are two kinds of music? No, not teenage music and adult music. No, not even secular music and religious music.

There's music for listening to.

And there's music for not listening to.

The second kind doesn't necessarily come only from teenagers, with their portable boom-boxes blasting out decibels. Think about the background music that plays in stores and offices and elevators. It's played and recorded so that you won't pay attention to it, so that it can influence you without your ever being aware of it.

For many of us, brought up in the Christian faith, Christianity has become a kind of background music. It's so familiar, it has been there so long, that we don't even notice it any more.

The question is, does it still have the power to influence us? Or do we just ignore it?

Waterfalls

The first time I saw Niagara Falls, I thought someone must turn it off at night. Otherwise, I thought, there would be nothing left for people to watch the next day.

There were always people watching the Falls. Night or day, rain or shine, people leaned on railings to watch the green water sluice over the edge and plunge into the gorge below.

A waterfall – almost any waterfall – has a strange fascination for us. We can stand for hours, sometimes, watching the water fall free in endlessly varying patterns...

Subconsciously, perhaps, we identify with waterfalls. Like our lives, waterfalls never stand still. They keep changing. They never repeat; the water that's there this second is not the same water that was there a second before. A waterfall is constantly being reborn. There's a restlessness about waterfalls that we know too well.

Above the fall, the stream is tightly confined by banks, constricted by channels. We feel the same way about life. And then suddenly, like a waterfall, we are set free. Sometimes that freedom is frightening It's a long way down to the bottom. Sometimes it's exhilarating.

But waterfalls must be constantly replenished from their source to keep flowing. So must our faith. Or, like a waterfall, we too will dry up and die.

Felt pen

I got a felt pen out of our kitchen drawer the other day. I wanted to label an envelope, with big fat letters and dark black ink, so that even the most visually-challenged postal clerk couldn't miss it.

And it had dried up.

I don't know how long it had been lying inside that kitchen drawer, unused, untouched, forgotten. Too long, apparently.

The stuff that makes the ink in felt pens so smelly, the stuff that evaporates quickly so that the black marks won't smear and smudge, had evaporated.

As I sat there, scraping the paper with a hardened nib, I wondered how often that happens to people's faith. You come out of a religious experience all juiced up, ready to write your message on the world around you. But the time isn't quite right. So you set your enthusiasm aside for a while. You put it away in a drawer, until the right time comes.

And when the time comes, you find it's all dried up.

Shells

Hardly anyone can resist collecting shells along a beach. Watch folks strolling along the sands, picking up a shell here, a shell there, holding it up to the light, turning it over in their hands...

A shell is small and fragile, easily broken. Yet when you hold it the right way so that it catches the light, its mother-of-pearl shines beautifully. Sometimes we too feel small and fragile, and easily broken. But when we catch the light the right way, we too can be unexpectedly beautiful.

Often the outside of a shell is grey and ugly; the beauty is hidden inside. So too with us.

Shells grow. Under a microscope, a shell's layers and rings reveal its age. The growth marks on shells are not obvious to the naked eye, any more than they are apparent on us. Some of our experiences are happy, some tragic. Yet every experience leaves its mark on us, too.

The marks are invisible, but they are there. They are our growth rings. Without them, we would have to stay very small.

Fence

Farmers build fences to keep animals in; neighbors build fences to keep animals out. Whatever the reason for building a fence, it divides. It separates this side from that side. And as the old saying goes, the far side always looks greener.

I saw a fence in the Fraser Valley, outside of Vancouver. Cattle had cropped the grass inside the fence right down to the ground. The grass outside the fence wasn't actually any greener, but it was much longer. Some of the cows had stretched their necks – painfully, I'm sure – through the strands of barbed wire to gather as much of the fresh grass as they could reach.

I've never really liked fences. I don't like having limits imposed on me. I don't like being told that's as far as I can go. Especially when it comes to ideas, understandings, or concepts.

There's a fence between humans and God. We humans are not God; we never will be; we cannot aspire to be. As the prophet Isaiah quoted God: "My ways are not your ways, neither are my thoughts your thoughts."

I know I can't cross that fence. But forgive me, please, if I try to stretch through it as far as I can reach.

VCR

We bought our VCR at a discount electronic warehouse. The instruction manual was missing from the box when we got it.

"Don't worry," the slick young salesman assured us. "I'll order one for you. But you won't need it. I can almost guarantee you that you'll have it figured out for yourself before the manual arrives."

He didn't order it. And we didn't figure it out. After a while, we gave up trying.

To this day, most of the teeny-weeny buttons hiding behind a miniscule flip-down panel remain mysteries to us.

Sometimes I speak – a bit contemptuously, I fear – about people trying to get along on a "Sunday school" faith. I don't mean to denigrate Sunday school. But they're like us and our VCR – they've been introduced to a pretty powerful tool. But they left the manual back in the warehouse, and they spend most of their adult lives trying to figure out for themselves which buttons to push.

In fact, most of them give up trying.

I still wish I'd had a manual to help us use our VCR. I'm grateful that I had a "manual" – in the church and the Bible – to help me learn to live my faith.

Coffee urn

Coffee urns squat on counters like shiny fire hydrants with indigestion. They gurgle and burp, and burgle and gurp, and eventually produce a more or less drinkable fluid.

We can learn a lot about spiritual growth from coffee urns. Like them, we only produce something valuable when we're plugged in to a source of power. For the coffee urn, it's electricity; for the Christian, it's God.

Like urns, we may make a fair amount of unseemly noise while doing our thing. God's insights may come in silence, like a still small voice on a mountaintop. But before we can hear that still small voice, we have to climb the mountain – usually with as much grace as a drunken hippo. The noises we make, as we struggle upwards, may disturb others.

But, like coffee urns, we should be judged not on our noises but on the quality of life that we produce.

The urn needs pure water to make good coffee. We need to clean up our act, too – we can't produce good deeds with soiled motives.

In an urn, water filters through the coffee grounds, and comes out changed. Our lives, filtered through the grounds of experience, also come out changed.

No two urns of coffee ever come out identical, because they depend on the coffee grounds they pass through. And so no two Christians ever come out identical, because they are each colored by their experience and culture.

Door hinge

They're the most overlooked part of any door – the hinges. Yet without them, the door won't work at all.

Most of us become aware of hinges only when they fail. They squeak, or stick, or come loose. Then we oil them, or tighten their screws.

Most of us only become aware of the importance of our faith when it fails us, too. Otherwise, we take it for granted, like door hinges. We think that what we learned in Sunday school or Bible class, years ago, is still in good shape. Until some day it sticks, or squeaks, or jams.

There are, of course, those who insist that faith of any kind is unnecessary. Irrelevant. An anachronism in a post-modern society – whatever that may mean.

It's interesting that on most doors, you can only see the hinges from one side. From the inside. From the outside, the hinge is invisible. Maybe that's why people on the outside of our churches don't think faith matters.

Shining light on the Bible

To a people accustomed to telling their story by saying, "Once we were slaves in Egypt..." Jesus told present-day parables. He told about people getting mugged and robbed on a journey, about merchants buying and selling, about losing and finding something valuable, about bread and wine and seeds and yeast. Commonplace, ordinary, everyday things. So our psalms [and parables] need to be about everyday things too.

None of this denies the validity of the Bible. or seeks to replace it—any more than Jesus' message denied or replaced the Hebrew scriptures, the only Bible he knew. It simply provides alternative images.

–from Everyday Psalms, *(Wood Lake Books, 1994). p. 6*

◆　　◆　　◆

In any group, a certain number of parables will deal with the Bible. Some simply affirm it as the dependable word of God – more or less infallible or accurate according to the doctrinal leanings of the participants.

But a surprising number of parables cast new light on the Bible itself, helping to make sense out of verses that might otherwise prove troubling or just bewildering.

Picnic cooler

It always seemed a bit unfair of the writer of Revelation, traditionally known as John of Patmos, to tell the little church in Laodicea: "Because you are lukewarm – neither hot nor cold – I will spit you out of my mouth."

After all, who wants to be cold and hostile? And you can't be hot all the time, can you? Everyone needs a rest now and then...

Then a group creating parables considered a picnic cooler.

Picnic coolers are supposed to keep hot things hot, and cool things cool, they explained. But sometimes the insulation in a picnic cooler wears out. You put something hot into your old picnic cooler, and when you want to use it, it comes out lukewarm. Or you put something cold into the cooler, and it comes out lukewarm too. Then you know it's time to get rid of that cooler and get a new one that works better.

What's true for picnic coolers is true for our faith, too, they concluded. When our faith leaves us only lukewarm, neither hot nor cold, it's probably time to junk some old ideas, or trade them in on some new ideas and insights that work better.

Garlic

"You are the salt of the earth," Jesus told his disciples. I wonder if he knew about garlic.

Garlic would have made just as memorable a metaphor as salt.

Like salt, garlic adds flavor to food. Like salt, a little bit of garlic goes a long way. In fact, just like salt, too much garlic can make food inedible.

But garlic has a few special qualities of its own that salt doesn't. Salt is secretive; garlic is public. If you add salt to your food, no one can tell how much you used. If you add garlic, everyone will know. Especially if the garlic user happens to stand beside you or the bus.

There's only one way to disguise garlic breath. That's for everyone to have some garlic. Including the stranger on the bus. In that sense, garlic is much more democratic than salt!

Garlic also does something else that salt can't. It can reproduce itself. Salt is a mineral, inert, lifeless. Salt will never create more salt. But if you plant some garlic cloves, in a few months you'll have more.

Like the Christian faith itself, there's a mystery to garlic. When you look at it first, it looks like a unit, complete, take-it-or-leave-it. But when you look closer, you'll find you can peel off its layers. There's more inside than you expected. In fact, when you open up a garlic bulb fully, you'll find many cloves inside. The one is many! Think of them as Father, Son, and Holy Spirit; as Creator, Redeemer, and Sustainer; as Mother, Lover, and Friend – it matters not what names you apply – the amazing thing is that a single unity can contain such diversity.

Yet they're all the same garlic.

"You are the garlic of the earth." It has a nice ring, doesn't it?

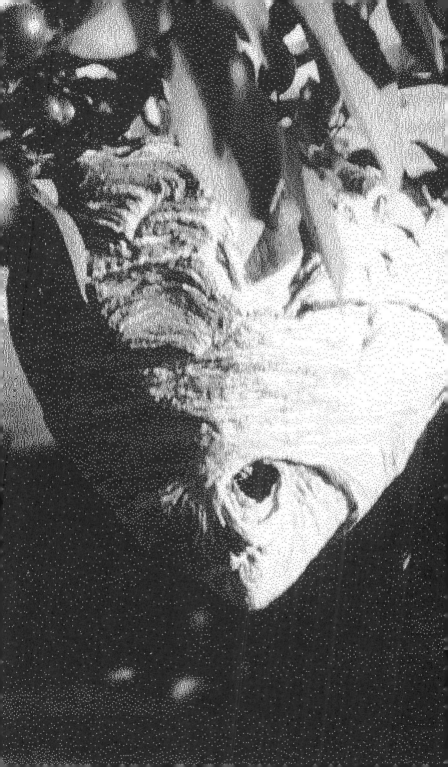

Wasp nest

Once, when I was a boy, I climbed a tree that had a wasps' nest in it. Of course, I didn't know there was a wasps' nest there – until I bumped into it with my head.

After that discovery, I came down the tree very quickly!

Having had a close acquaintance with a nest, however, I've retained a kind of personal interest in wasps. A few years ago, on a hike in the woods, I came across an abandoned nest sliced almost in half. I was amazed at the wasps' engineering. Layer upon layer, the nest evolved from sheets of wasp-made paper, one sheet laid on top of the other, the whole structure gradually growing in complexity and importance.

Rather like the Bible, I suppose.

Once upon a time, what our society calls the Bible consisted of only a few books, now known as the Torah – the books of the Hebrew people's Exodus from Egypt and the laws they developed to govern their behavior as they wandered around out there in the desert.

Over time, other people wrote down the stories of their encounters with God. People recorded histories and songs. They recounted ancient myths and legends about their dim and distant ancestors. About 2,000 years ago, another group added stories about a man named Jesus, and a collection of letters sent between Jesus' followers.

With each addition, each new sheet of paper or parchment, the whole thing grew in complexity and worth.

Water

North Americans don't like to admit we're well off. We read Jesus' assertion that "it is harder for the rich to enter the kingdom of heaven than for a camel to pass through the eye of a needle," and we look for excuses. It was an exaggeration, we say. It was a joke, a sample of Jesus' humor. And he couldn't have meant us, because we're not really rich. Look at how much vanishes in taxes, in mortgage payments, in grocery bills, even in holidays and travel. We lament either how much our cars cost, or how we have to put up with some old clunker.

Yet we all water our lawns.

To most of the world, the surest sign of our affluence must be our scandalous waste of the most valuable substance on earth. No, that substance is not gold, platinum, or even two-inch tenderloin steaks. It's water. You can live without precious metals for a lifetime; you can live without food for weeks if necessary; you can't go more than a day or two without water.

Most of the world measures its water in cupfuls. A family will consider itself fortunate to have, perhaps, five gallons a day – for drinking, for washing, for hygiene, for everything. We flush that much every time we empty our toilet tanks.

Compared to the rest of the world, our use of water brands us as unbelievably wealthy. Our lack of awareness of that wealth, our refusal to admit our privileged position, casts a new light on passing through the eye of a needle.

Jigsaw puzzles

When you first dump a jigsaw puzzle out onto a table, it looks like a hopeless mess. At first glance, nothing matches. Nothing fits together. And the bigger the puzzle, the more hopeless the task seems.

The Bible is like a jigsaw puzzle with an infinite number of pieces. It has 66 books, assembled by an unknown number of writers and editors. Each book has hundreds of messages.

When you first dump open the Bible to see what you've got, it looks like a hopeless mess. All those bits and pieces don't seem to match with other bits and pieces. Initially, you try to make sense out of a verse here and a verse there – like trying to find a corner or an edge in a jigsaw puzzle.

But once you start putting pieces together, it starts to make more sense.

And the more pieces you put together, the better it looks.

Concrete

Sand and gravel are unstable substances. It's hard work, walking on a gravel beach or climbing a sand dune. The grains beneath your feet won't stick together. They yield to every pressure. They slide. They slip.

But add cement and water and those same unstable grains turn into concrete. Sand and gravel and powdered limestone bind together permanently.

The Kingdom of God is like that, Jesus would probably tell us today. Without adherence to the will of God, we're like that loose sand and gravel. We're as unstable as a house would be, built on a sandbar in the middle of a river. We yield to every pressure of the world around us. We slip and slide, and generally go downhill.

But add the unifying presence of God, and all those loose elements of our lives are bound together in a common purpose. And what had been so unstable that it yielded to every whim and fad becomes so strong that it can support great loads under great stress. It's as strong as a rock, strong enough to support any house.

Cottonwoods

Once upon a time, God set out to sow some seeds.

So God created the cottonwood tree. And when the seeds were ready to be scattered, they filled the air with fluff.

Some of the seeds fell on the paved roads and the asphalt parking lots. And the cars drove over them, and crushed them.

Some of the seeds fell on the rocks and the gravel along the shore. When the water wetted them, they sprouted and sprang up. But because they had no earth in which to sink their roots, they quickly withered and died.

And some of the seeds fell among the weeds. And because the thorns and the thistles grew more quickly than the cottonwood shoots, they shut off the sun and the rain, and the little shoots died.

But a few of the seeds landed on good soil along the river banks. And the seeds sent their roots deep into the moist earth, and grew tall and strong, until they were able to send out their own seeds.

And God saw that it was good.

Wooden spoon

When our children were young – back in the days when parents still thought they should enforce obedience with physical discipline – we used to use a wooden spoon as a threat. I don't think we ever actually used it on our children.

But one time, when my patience was running thin, I whacked the wooden spoon vigorously against my own leg. It hurt. It hurt a lot more than I had expected. But the result was even more unexpected.

The spoon shattered. Pieces of it flew around the room.

And our kids were terrified. In the breaking of the spoon, they recognized the lengths to which punishment might go. They scurried off to bed without a trace of protest.

I don't know – and there's no way I ever can know – how much the Crucifixion hurt God. I suspect it might have hurt more than God expected.

But it had a powerful effect. People didn't have to experience the crucifixion themselves to realize how badly things could go wrong. And how far God was prepared to go to share our sufferings with us.

Church community

It would be nice if God simply talked to us in plain English. Then we would have no trouble living in the Kingdom under God's will.

But I sometimes suspect that God doesn't speak English. Maybe God doesn't use words at all – except, perhaps, in emergencies. After all, if God spoke clearly in words, why would there be so much disagreement among the churches? Shouldn't we all be hearing the same thing?

– from Two Worlds in One, *(Wood Lake Books, 1985), p. 61*

•   •   •

People relate best to other people. So it shouldn't be surprising that a great many of the parables that people create deal with their relationships with other people, in the church or out of it.

Some of the parables they make up bring on howls of laughter when they neatly skewer opponents. I haven't included any of those – though I wonder, sometimes, if some of Jesus' parables might not also have skewered unpopular people well known to his hearers.

Some parables about the church community deal with leadership, some with learning. But behind them lies a common theme: there is purpose and value in belonging to this community.

Sandpaper

Sandpaper brings out the natural beauty in wood. You use it to smooth the wood before you apply varnish; you can use it also to smooth the coats of varnish, to build up a deep and glowing finish.

Yet sandpaper does its job by being abrasive. Sandpaper is rough stuff. It works by scratching and scouring. The secret to sandpaper is knowing just how much roughness to use. Too coarse a paper will destroy a fine finish; too fine a paper will never grind down the rough spots.

Sandpaper can teach us how to handle people, too.

Sometimes being soft and gentle with people doesn't work. To bring out their natural but well-hidden beauty, we may sometimes have to be abrasive, tough, difficult – even though we would rather use kid gloves and soft words.

The same treatment may destroy others. It may permanently scar the polish they have taken years to build up.

Just as we should never use coarser sandpaper than necessary on wood, we should never be more abrasive than necessary with people, or we may damage them.

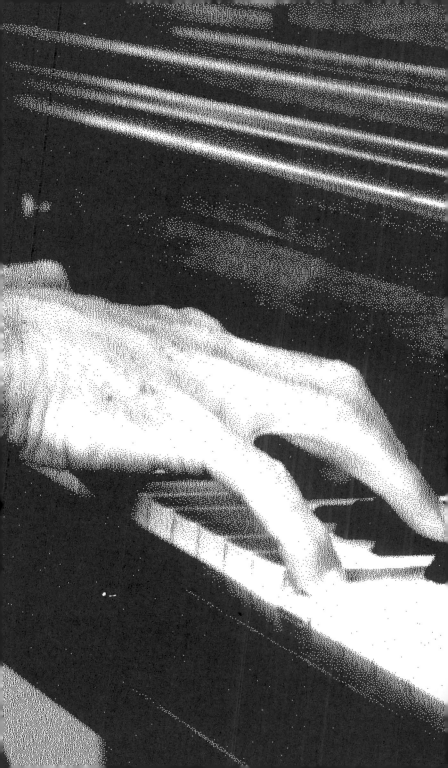

Piano

A piano could be a lesson in racial harmony. It has black keys and white keys. They have to work together to make music.

A piano could be a lesson in pop psychology. Like any stringed instrument, it can make music only when its strings are under tension. That message could comfort people who fear tension tearing them apart.

But the message I like best came from a group who noted that each key on a piano can play only one note. Just one. "We humans like to think of ourselves as independent," the group said. "We want to be jacks-of-all-trades, self-sufficient. The piano reminds us that it's enough to be able to play one note, as long as we play it in tune. Then the musician can use us to make beautiful harmony."

That's why we gather in congregations, they suggested. So that each of us can play the note that each plays best, and God can use us to make beautiful music.

Sliced bread

My mother had a terrible time slicing bread. The harder she concentrated on the loaf, the more each slice veered off the vertical.

The correction, when it eventually became necessary, produced one slice that resembled the wedge one sticks under a door to hold it open.

I've wondered, sometimes, why one person can slice bread straight, and another can't. I think it has something to do with having an external point of reference. I know, when I slice bread, that I need to line the knife up with something vertical – a door frame, a counter edge, a window. That external reference keeps the cut true.

My mother, I think, concentrated on the loaf itself. She tried to line up each slice parallel to the last slice. But if the last slice was off true, the next slice was more so. The effect of every variation, no matter how slight, was cumulative. Things got worse; they never corrected themselves.

The same happens to us, when we focus exclusively on our own experience. Each action is based on what we've done before. Each deviation from truth, from rightness, may be fractional, but it's cumulative.

Until, eventually, we find ourselves tilted so far off true that we fall down.

The only answer is to have something – or someone – who is absolutely dependable. Someone external, other than ourselves. Someone we can line ourselves up with.

There are many reasons for belonging to a church. But perhaps the most basic is to line ourselves up with the most reliable standard for human behavior that we know, a person we call Jesus of Nazareth.

Pay telephone

Anyone can see a connection between prayer and telephones. It's easy to say that praying is like calling God – though I suspect that for many people, a busy signal or no answer feels more common than a good long heart-to-heart conversation. Sometimes you get through, sometimes you don't.

And some people have lost God's number. Or never had it.

Some other people just call any number, hoping to get an answer. From anyone.

But what would you say about a pay telephone?

A pay telephone adds a new dimension. It reminds us that there's a cost to prayer. You have to invest something of yourself before you can hope to get an answer.

Fire extinguisher

At university, many of our fire extinguishers were just cans of water with a hand pump on top.

On our boat, we had a fire extinguisher that blew a white powder at any blaze. Some neighborhood children got hold of it one day, and covered both boat and yard with what would, in winter, have looked like snow.

When I set up an office in our basement, some years ago, our daughter bought me a special fire extinguisher. It produced nothing but gas to quench fires. Because, as the sales clerk explained to her, "If your dad gets powder or water or anything else into his computer's hard drive, it'll be just as cooked as if the fire got it."

All fire extinguishers put out fires. But each kind of fire requires its own kind of extinguisher. Water will put out a fire in wood or paper, but will make an electrical or an oil fire worse. Airports need foam, to reduce the risk of a skidding airplane causing sparks that could ignite fuel.

Old-time preachers used to thunder about the fire and brimstone of hell. They offered Jesus Christ as a kind of universal fire extinguisher.

Many people still do. They haven't realized that different kinds of fires call for different solutions. By simply spraying a one-size-fits-all Jesus at every human conflagration, they may intensify some fires.

Cucumber

The churches in one area felt discouraged.

Some theologically-conservative congregations in their area were making a splash. They had television and radio programs. They held youth rallies and evangelistic crusades. At Christmas, their massed choirs formed a Christmas tree and sold videotapes of themselves singing carols. People flocked in. But almost all the money those people gave stayed in the local area, to make the congregations even more attractive.

The other churches were smaller, and less flamboyant. Their members didn't have a whole lot of time for outreach committees and door-to-door evangelism, because they were already involved in Big Brothers and Elizabeth Fry and the Hemophilia Society. They gave generously to their church, though, and particularly to their national mission fund, which supported partner churches in Africa and India and South America. But nobody gave them much credit for what they were doing. And so they felt discouraged.

Then they meditated on, of all things, the lowly cucumber. And they felt better.

Because, they realized, the cucumber vine has a very showy flower. It's bright colored, superficially attractive, and stands proud of itself in the sunlight. But by itself, it's useless.

The valuable part of a cucumber is not very attractive at all. It dwells in the shadows, down with the dirt and the roots. You may have to look hard to find it, turning over the leaves and ignoring the bright flowers.

To savor a cucumber, you may have to get your hands dirty. But it's the only thing that makes a cucumber vine worth having.

Orange or banana

You can't really tell what an orange or a banana is like until you peel it.

Sometimes a banana looks fine on the outside. But when you peel it, you find it bruised and rotten inside, unfit for eating.

Sometimes an orange looks green on the outside, but turns out to be sweet and juicy inside.

In the same way, people look at local churches from the outside. They make judgments about the architect, the grounds, the parking lot. But you can never know what a congregation is like until you get inside. Not just by stepping inside the doors and looking around. But by taking the risk of peeling it open, and tasting the fruit itself. By taking the time to find out what the people are like, and what they believe, and how they live those beliefs.

Not all oranges peel the same way. Some have skins that slip off easily; with some, you have to work hard to get inside.

Congregations can be like that too.

Potato

We played a "Potato Game" with our older Sunday school group, some years ago.

Immigrants had been moving into the area. We had heard comments like, "All these Orientals look the same to me – I can't tell them apart!"

One of the teens brought in a bag of potatoes. Just ordinary potatoes. He handed out one to each member.

"They all look the same, don't they?" he said. "I want you to look at your potato really carefully. Get to know its size, its shape, all of its dimples and scars and marks."

Everyone stared intently at their potato. Some turned their potato over thoughtfully in their hands. A few giggled.

"Now talk to the person next to you. Show them how your potato is special and different from the other potato."

People gathered in pairs. A hum of conversation filled the room.

"Now the two of you turn to two others. And show each of them what makes your potato unique."

The hum grew louder.

After about ten minutes, the leader called everyone together. "Okay," he instructed the group, "throw your potatoes back into the bag."

He shook the bag, and then poured all the potatoes out into a pile on the floor. "Now," he said, "find **your** potato!"

And you know something? Every one of us could!

"If you can do that with potatoes," he announced, "you can do it with people. If you think all people look the same, it's because you haven't taken the time to really get to know them."

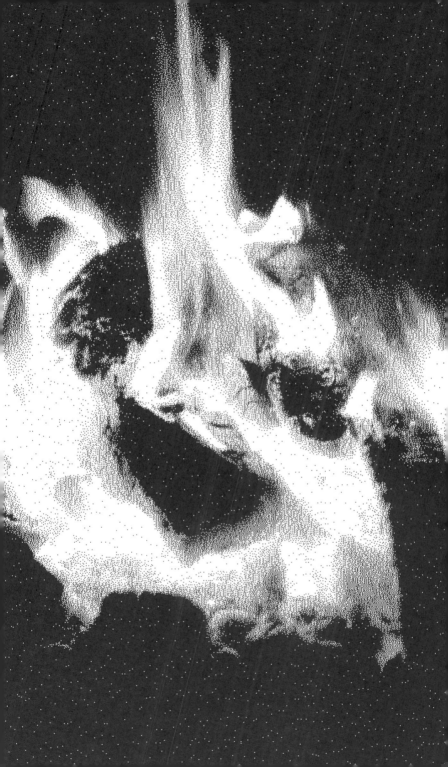

Campfire

The flicker of flame in a campfire is hypnotic. The light itself dances, playing with your imagination. Around a campfire, there's no need for conversation – so conversation often flows more freely.

You can sit for hours, watching the coals glow and crackle. But if you pull one of those embers out of the fire, it soon grows cold and black.

That's probably why we need to gather in communities. Each of us can glow individually. But without the reinforcement of others glowing around us, we too can grow cold.

Any kind of people who share similar goals and ideals will serve as community. But the gathering of those who think of themselves as the people of God, the congregation or parish, has some special qualities.

For as long as humans have existed, fire has been a symbol for God. God spoke to Moses out of a burning bush, to the followers of Jesus in tongues of flame.

The warmth reaches out like a hug. And like a warning. For fire can burn, as well as warm; it can destroy, as well as give life. Fire, in that sense, is a good symbol of God's spirit – for God's spirit can give new life, but it can also destroy the old life.

Stone wall

The community of faith is like a stone wall.

Skilled hands craft stone walls. Each wall is made up of many different stones, of many shapes, sizes, kinds, and colors. Yet combined, they form one wall. A well-built wall is solid, withstanding both weather and time. Sun and rain, hail and snow, cannot break it down.

Yet sometimes walls do fall apart. The bond that connects one stone to another weakens. A stone falls out, and leaves a gap. Unless the wall is repaired, more stones will loosen and fall away, until the wall itself collapses in ruins.

Peter, in a letter preserved in the Bible, describes the followers of Jesus as "living stones."

Like walls, churches and congregations need maintenance. When people fall away, the gaps need to be repaired. Sometimes the missing stones can be found and brought back; sometimes they have to be replaced with new stones, and all the other stones adjusted to help the new addition fit better.

Combs

Combs come in all shapes and sizes. Small combs hide inside a pocket or purse; big combs advertise their presence with flamboyant colors and shapes. Some combs are straight, others are curved. Some are stuck in drawers, some are stuck in hair.

But in fact, all combs have only one purpose – to discipline unruly hair. To train it, to guide it, to shape it, to keep it in place.

Combs are like Christian communities. We call them parishes and congregations; we meet in chapels and churches and cathedrals. But they all have only one purpose – to discipline Christians. "Discipline" doesn't mean to punish or judge; it comes from the same root as "disciple."

You can – as Sunday morning golfers love to proclaim – worship God on a golf course. Or beside a trout stream. Or on a high and windy hill. But you will never, in any of those places, have your unruly reactions held up to scrutiny, or have your complacent convictions challenged, or have your apathy transformed into committed action.

We need the community of Christians to train us, to guide us, to shape us, to keep us in place.

Porridge

For some 20 years, my mother made me porridge for breakfast. Every morning. Winter and summer. "It'll stick to your ribs," she told me cheerfully.

As a child, I used to feel my ribs, to see if anything had stuck to them inside. It took me a long time to realize she was speaking figuratively, not literally.

I've been going to church for almost 60 years now. I go for the same reason I ate my mother's porridge all those years. To get nourishment. Spiritual nourishment, in this case – but every Sunday, I hope some of it will stick to me (figuratively, of course).

There's a lot of similarity between porridge and church attendance. Both are best when you receive them warm. In the bowl, with the warmth of the stove; in church, with the warmth of friendship.

Both can be pretty bland when they're too uniform. I preferred the crunch and variety of Red River Cereal® to the smooth uniformity of Cream of Wheat® and I still prefer churches that encourage a diversity of views – even a touch of heresy now and then – to those that expect strict conformity to their standards.

Sometimes, of course, porridge has a few lumps in it. So does belonging to a faith community.

Shoe laces

Have you ever tried to write out instructions for tying shoe laces? "Pass the right lace over the left, then tuck it under and bring it back up again... Loop the left lace, which is now on the right, back on itself. Now cross the right lace, which is on the left, over the left lace, which is on the right, and then tuck it..."

The process is almost impossible to describe. There's only way to learn how to tie shoe laces. That's to do it, with someone else holding your hand and guiding your fingers through all those complex maneuvers. Tying your own shoe laces, without help, used to be a major achievement in kindergarten, I recall.

It's like so much of life. We can be told, over and over, how to do things. We can read instructions. But the only way to learn the impossibly complicated maneuvers of getting along with others in an increasingly crowded world is to do it. And it works best if you have someone holding your hand, guiding your reactions.

Almost any adult can guide a child's fingers in learning to tie shoe laces. But adults, who themselves are still learning how to get along with others, need their own guide.

That's why we turn, instinctively, to religion. Each religion has its own guide. Buddhists look to Gautama Buddha; Hindus to Krishna or some other manifestation of deity; Muslims to Mohammed; Christianity offers Jesus of Nazareth.

Stapler

Staplers may be the most overlooked item on desks. On my desk, the stapler often gets buried beneath stray sheets of paper. I don't miss it until I need something to fasten some of those sheets of paper together. Then I begin slapping the sheets of paper until something lumpy underneath goes "ka-chunk." That's how I find the stapler.

I hate to admit it, but in some ways, my faith is rather like that stapler. When things are going well, when I'm busy, my faith gets overlooked. I take it for granted. Like a stapler, it keeps important pieces of my life together – but often I don't turn to my faith, my convictions about the way life should be lived, until I find that things are in danger of drifting apart.

Sometimes, when I find the stapler, I discover it's run out of staples. Then no amount of pounding on it will fasten anything together. My faith needs periodic refills too. The refills may be small things, as insignificant as the bits of wire that make the staples themselves: a conversation with a friend, a potluck supper, a word of wisdom in a sermon, a joyful hymn, a Bible study, an opportunity to work together...

Yet it's these little things that bind together a group of people who share certain ideals, beliefs, and convictions.

Crutch

I broke a bone in my foot, one evening. Joan, my spouse, rushed me to the emergency ward. I came back with crutches.

No one likes crutches. They're ugly. They're awkward. They're uncomfortable. After a few hours on crutches, my arms ached, and my armpits felt as if they'd been rubbed raw. Crutches can even be a hazard – have you ever tried going through a revolving door with crutches sticking out either side?

Yet I would have been much worse off without those crutches than with them.

I hear religion referred to with scorn as a crutch. The scorn implies that we should be able to do without crutches; we should be able to stand on our feet without relying on ancient traditions of a God interacting with a chosen people.

No doubt it's better to walk than to hobble; it's better to stand on your own than to depend on crutches to hold you up.

But when you have a broken bone, or a broken heart, it's awfully comforting to have a crutch around.

Sometimes the church rubs me raw, too. But I think I'll keep it – for those times when I really need a crutch.

Casters

We put casters under refrigerators, or beds, or sofas, to make them easier to move. Isn't it a shame we can't put casters under some immovable people?

Did you ever notice? You never get one caster at a time. One caster, by itself, is about as useless as one leg of a pair of pliers. Or as one well-intentioned person, working alone.

Castors have to work in groups. So do Christians, if they expect to move immovable objects.

Doorknobs

Our dog can open doors. We have lever door handles. So he just rests a hairy paw on the lever, and, miraculously, the door opens.

We had a cat once that understood about doorknobs. It couldn't turn them, but it recognized that doorknobs somehow open doors, and so it rattled the doorknob when it wanted in or out.

Neither the cat nor the dog has any idea how a doorknob works. The mechanism is hidden. Even if they could see it, it would be incomprehensible to them.

No matter what the shape or size of doorknobs, they all have the same purpose. Levers or balls, wood or metal or plastic, warm or cold to the touch, they all exist only to open doors.

Perhaps Christians are like those doorknobs. We too come in many shapes and sizes. And some of us are warm or cold, when touched. We like to think we have lofty tasks to perform. But maybe all that matters is that we open doors – to life, to faith, to God – through which others may pass.

We don't need to know how it works. We just have to do it.

Lemonade

On a hot day, there's nothing more refreshing than a glass of icy lemonade.

To countless suffering people, the story of Jesus has come as refreshingly as lemonade. Refugees and slaves, victims of ill health and of war, have found comfort and consolation in the story of his crucifixion and resurrection. They have identified with an innocent man suffering for something he didn't do. They find hope in the message that the way things are isn't the only way things can be.

But for many in the more affluent world, the lemonade has gone sour. The good news has a bitter taste.

Some high-profile evangelists try to sweeten the mix. They disguise the bitterness with jazz and razzmatazz. They water down the natural tartness of the message and add artificial flavors.

Others know what's good for us. So they cut out the sugar. They give us the straight lemon, straight from the shoulder.

If the drink comes in a glass emblazoned with warning labels against everything from genocide to having fun, who's going to find it refreshing? If the drink is offered with a sour face, who's going to taste it?

Is it possible that the problem is not the lemonade, but the vendor?

Rope

The engineering students at university had their own version of Newton's laws of mechanics:

1. For every action, there is an equal and opposite reaction.
2. You can't push a rope.

The first law is more or less as Isaac Newton expressed it; the second was supposed to be humorous. In fact, those two "laws" contained many of the essential truths of engineering.

They're also a fairly good summary of social and political life. Especially the second. For you can't push people along from behind, any more than you can push a rope.

The best way to move people is from out in front, pulling.

Perhaps that's why Jesus of Nazareth, when he gathered his first disciples, told them, "Follow me."

Treasures in new earthen vessels

The prophet Jeremiah used parables with great skill. He compared God to a potter who discarded a clay pot that wasn't shaping up properly, and started over again. "Can I not do with you, Israel, as the potter does with his clay?" God asked, through Jeremiah. (18:1–6)

— from Two Worlds in One, *(Wood Lake Books, 1985), p. 74*

♦　　　♦　　　♦

By far the largest majority of parables created by church groups fall into a category that might be called, "Treasures in earthen pots."

Paul coined the metaphor, in his second letter to the Corinthians (4:7). He intended it to apply to the divine message, conveyed by frail and fallible human bodies. My parable-writers applied it to things.

Appearances can be deceiving, they said. It's what's inside that matters.

Most of the parables in this section, then, deal with objects that are very easy to overlook, objects of little value in themselves. Yet they cannot be judged only on their own merit. For without these "earthen pots," there might be no treasure.

Like God the potter, who discards the old which no longer functions, and creates anew, we need constantly to create new earthen vessels to hold God's truths.

Earrings

Lois Huey Heck wears the most creative earrings I know. There have been many stories written about Lois – as a designer and artist, as a single mother, as a wife struggling with the reality of a brain-damaged husband – but none, as far as I know, about Lois's earrings.

She makes many of her earrings herself. One time, she came in with earrings made out of rust. She'd been to her family homestead, and salvaged some scraps of sheet iron, rusted through like a sieve, brown with time. Lacquered, suspended from hooks, what had been trash glowed like a rose.

Lois has a rare gift. She can see beauty in the debris and detritus of life.

All Christians claim to have that gift. For at the center of our faith lies the Cross. An innocent man was executed by being nailed to a gallows on a hill where dogs and vultures fought over the remains of the discarded dead. We Christians tell the world that something beautiful happened in that hideous torture.

But I wonder if we really see it. Or if only a few people like Lois can really see a jewel in that garbage heap.

Frost

Every winter, the road from our house into town disintegrates. Frost heaves up patches of the blacktop, which quickly burst into axle-jarring potholes.

Every winter, someone's car quits. Frost reduces the power of the car's battery. We have to get the jumper cables out again. Maybe we have to buy a new battery.

Every winter, the path down the hill below our house freezes into a sheet of ice. The trail to the post office becomes so treacherous it should be reported to our life insurance company.

It would be very easy to hate frost.

We give it a bad name, in fact. We talk of getting a "frosty reception," of being "frozen out."

Yet it's frost that keeps the food in our freezer from rotting. It was frost that ground down the mountains and gouged the valleys that contain our lakes. It was frost that split the ancient rocks and began reducing them to sand and gravel and soil. It is still frost that breaks up the hard lumps of soil to make it hospitable for next spring's seeds. Frost stores moisture, and causes the sap to run in the trees.

We should be grateful for frost.

Perhaps we should be grateful, too, for the cold snaps of life. It's easy to curse the tragedy of a death, of a job loss, of a separation or divorce. And with good reason; they're as unpleasant as freezing your tongue to a fence post.

But perhaps, like the frost, they may be blessings in disguise. We have to wait for spring, to see.

Garbage

Every life has some garbage in it. Live frugally if you will; reduce, reuse, and recycle as much as you can – even so, there will always be a certain amount of waste to get rid of.

If you can't get rid of it, it piles up. Eventually, that garbage will choke you. It will destroy you.

For a quarter of a century, we lived in a municipality that had garbage strikes every couple of years. As sure as contracts run out, the yellow trucks quit rumbling down our street. Bags of garbage littered the curbs and piled up in the parks. Discarded sofas and broken bedframes blossomed on front lawns and parking lots.

Garbage is kind of like sin, that way. Nobody's perfect – at least, no current human is. Everyone has a sin here, a sin there. Not much, perhaps. But unless we can get rid of it, it piles up. The accumulation of little sins stifles us. It takes over our lives, as evident as an abandoned refrigerator at the end of the driveway.

Historically, the church has offered many ways of disposing of that garbage. Confession is one. "Come unto me, all you who are weary and heavy laden," Jesus is reported as saying. "Cast your cares upon Jesus," say evangelicals.

In a sense, that's a service God performs for us. Like a big yellow garbage truck, God comes around to help us clean up our lives and make them livable again.

But unlike the big yellow garbage trucks, God never goes on strike.

Erasers

If you want to know about forgiveness, think of erasers. Unlike ballpoint pens, which are extremely judgmental, erasers give you a chance to correct your mistakes and do better.

But don't confuse forgiving with forgetting. When erasers forgive, they don't undo whatever you did. The impression is still there in the paper; the marks of your mistake can still be traced by those who want to find them.

Forgiveness doesn't give you a clean sheet of paper, to start over with. The past is still present.

But by using an eraser, you imply a commitment to improve. There's no point in erasing a spelling error and then repeating the word the same way. You erase because you realize where you went wrong, and now you want to get it right.

Forgiveness doesn't wipe the slate clean either. It doesn't undo what you did. And it's not approval for what you did. It helps you see where you went wrong, and gives you another chance to get it right.

Kleenex®

When I was a child, I carried a cloth handkerchief with me everywhere. I haven't carried a handkerchief for years.

Now there's a box of tissues in every bathroom, every kitchen, every office. I take them for granted. When I have to blow my nose, I don't even ask the owners of the box if I may use one of their tissues. I just take it. I'd never do that with a handkerchief tucked into someone's purse or pocket.

That's how common tissues have become. In fact, the makers of Kleenex® and other tissues go to great lengths to protect their investment. They trademark the name, to prevent it from becoming simply a generic description.

If Christianity were just being introduced, like a brand new invention, people might think it was a marvelous new way of life. That's what happened some 20 centuries ago.

We shouldn't take either Christianity or Kleenex for granted.

Kleenex pops up. So do Christians, often unexpectedly.

Kleenex dries your tears. The Christian faith has brought comfort to millions.

Kleenex wipes up spills. It cleans up messes. You toss it away into a wastebasket. Christianity offers the same good news to people burdened by guilt, or trapped into a damaging way of life – you can throw away the mess and make a fresh start.

There are dozens of other uses for tissues.

I wonder if we make as many uses of Christianity.

From Colleen Hurst To: J█████ Taylor

To:

D

FAX

I know that you mention
that this message finds you.

Pushpins and thumbtacks

My father, a former missionary, created this little parable about thumbtacks.

Thumbtacks, he noted, do many things. A thumbtack is very small. It may seem insignificant. But when you can't find one, you realize how important it is.

A thumbtack by itself is useless. In fact, it is dangerous, as anyone who has sat on or stepped on a thumbtack knows all too well. In the same way, any form of faith isolated from life can be useless at best, dangerous at worst. Those who rigidly separate their faith convictions from their work, or their politics, are as dangerous as a thumbtack lying loose.

Thumbtacks can be used as markers, or even as decoration. But mainly, they hold one thing to another thing. You can stick a thumbtack through many layers of paper. But it must always have a receptive layer, somewhere below, before it can sink in.

"That's just like the gospel," he continued, perhaps thinking of his experiences in India, "presented to people who do not already know about Jesus. Unless there is a receptive layer, somewhere, the message cannot sink in."

Pruning shears

I don't like pruning plants. That's partly because I don't really know much about what I'm doing. I trim a bit of this and a bit of that, and maybe the plant looks better afterwards. Or maybe it doesn't.

It's also because I suspect that pruning must hurt the plant. For exactly that reason, I don't like the idea of someone pruning me.

Oh, I know that when Jesus said, "I am the vine, and God is the gardener. He cuts off every branch that doesn't bear fruit, and every branch that is fruitful he trims clean so that it will produce even more," he wasn't talking about God physically nipping off my fingers and toes.

But I'm quite attached to my work, my family, my pets, my possessions. I like having a small sports car to drive. I like having air conditioning in my house, and friends around me. I like most of my habits. Even some of my bad habits.

Perhaps I'm too attached to them. Some of them may be getting in the way of what God wants me to do and be.

Does a plant know that the pruning I do is for its own good, to help it grow stronger? Even if it does, I doubt if it welcomes the shears.

I hope God will be gentle with me.

Name tags

Name tags advertise the name we want to be known by.

Some people write only their first names on a name tag. Some write last names. Some put so much information on their tag it's harder to read than a business card on a distant mantelpiece.

Presumably, some people don't want to be known. They attach their tags way down low, at about belt level, or tuck it under a jacket. Either way, it's impossible – or at least embarrassing – to sneak a quick peek at the name to refresh your memory.

Funny. I've never yet seen anyone put their baptized name on a name tag.

Because, you see, when we're baptized, we're born into a new family. God's family. My name is no longer just James Taylor; in baptism, it becomes James Christian. And just as I had to learn the customs of the Taylor family as I grew up in it, so I had to learn the ways of the Christian family by growing up in it.

Don't we want our baptismal family known?

Onions

Many people have created parables for me about onions.

An onion's dry, scaly skin can be unattractive, just like some people – until you get to know them better.

The layers of an onion can be like the experiences we accumulate as we grow as Christians.

An onion is like yeast or salt – a little bit goes a long way in flavoring the whole stew.

Peeling onions can reduce you to tears – so can some Christians!

One woman going through a difficult time in her life decided she needed to spring clean her refrigerator. It was starting to smell a bit... At the back of the vegetable drawer, she found a gooey mess that had once been some onions. Holding her nose, she dumped the slimy stuff into the sink, and ran water on it to wash it down the drain. To her surprise, in the middle of the rot and decay, three small green shoots were growing.

She said: "God was telling me, in those onions, that spring was coming. New life was growing, even where all I could see was death and decay."

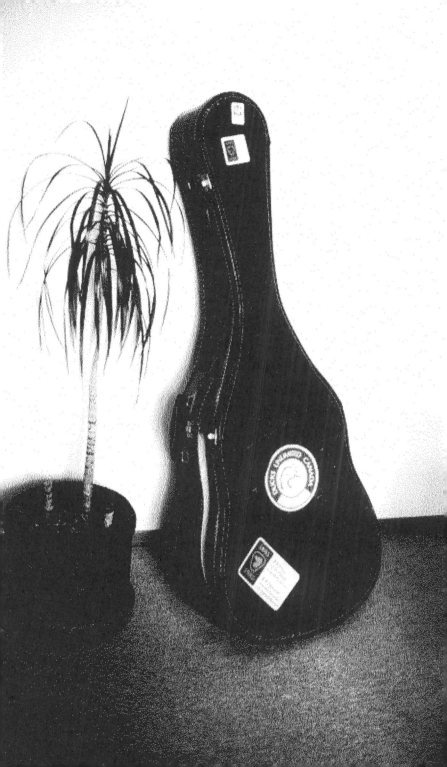

Guitar case

A guitar makes music. So does a clarinet, or a trombone, or a cello. And it's not hard to find analogies between one's faith and music.

But what about the case that carries the instrument? What good is it?

The case usually isn't beautiful. No one lavishes onto a mere violin case the care they'd give a Stradivarius.

Perhaps the music is like God. It's real – but it defies our definitions as patterns of sound waves. It has a life of its own, unique, different, moving us.

And some people are God's instruments. They make the music. They translate the music that permeates the universe into something we can hear and can respond to.

But not everyone can be a Stradivarius. There was only one Jesus.

The case protects the instrument. If Liona Boyd carried her guitar exposed – on the plane, on an escalator, through crowds in a department store – it would soon be reduced to kindling, incapable of making any more than a brief burst of fire. The case takes the beating, so that the instrument can continue to play.

Perhaps most of us are the guitar case. We get bounced around by life. We get battered, sometimes broken. But we enable the instrument to keep playing; we allow the music to be heard.

And when you open the case, you will find inside the impression left by the instrument that makes the music.

g their

eek,"

e ready

of all.

l eggs,
g
—Margl
l of

ator.

ng

ge A
n like

Please rewrite
←

Post-it® notes

I don't know how much money the 3M company has made off its little Post-it® notes; I'm not sure I want to know.

But I do know that it all started with a failure. 3M, of course, is Minnesota Mining and Manufacturing, makers of such indispensable things as Scotch tape®. They're always developing new adhesives that will stick stronger, firmer, longer...

One day, someone in their research lab mixed up a batch of glue that wouldn't stay stuck. It would hold a piece of paper in place, but the paper could be peeled off. They were about to discard this glue. Then someone started asking, "What use could we find for a glue that won't stick?" The rest is history.

Those Post-it notes have changed the way we think and act. As an editor, I stick them on manuscripts to query authors. Office staff stick them on memos, to supplement the information there. (One mother told me that she no longer makes shopping lists; when she notices something she will need, she simply sticks a Post-it onto the refrigerator. "It's a wonderful substitute for memory," she explained. "As long as you remember to check the notes as you head out the door.")

The Bible refers to Jesus as the "stone that the builders rejected" which becomes the cornerstone, the keystone in the arch, the crucial component in the whole structure of faith. The people of the Mediterranean had difficulty imagining that a person executed as a common criminal could be so important. The writers of the New Testament had to find an analogy, a metaphor, that described how a failure could become a foundation.

Most of us today don't deal much with cornerstones and keystones. But we all know about Post-it notes.

Snowbanks

A small group sat in Burton Avenue United Church in Barrie, writing personal parables. It was March. The buds on the trees were still dormant. Dirty grey piles of snow mounded the streets. Trickles of meltwater darkened the paving.

I told them: "Write a parable about those snowbanks."

First they noted the contrasts. The stuff that is currently ugly grey, compacted by time, used to be clean and fluffy white – a symbol for purity. It is now hard, and once was soft – a snowflake is often a symbol for lightness.

The snowflakes that create snowbanks go through a progression, a cycle. The water vapor that was originally a gas, becomes a solid, melts into a liquid, and eventually evaporates as a gas again. "Just like us," someone explained. "We start as spirit, become flesh, weaken, die, and return to our spirit nature."

Snowbanks are punctuation marks for the seasons; they mark the transition between winter and spring. Snowbanks look static, but they are always changing. They change as a result of the action of the sun. Some of us seem to be static, locked into our history – but we too may be constantly changing.

And someone described the snowbanks as the labor pains of winter giving birth to spring. They are the nourishment that seeps deep into the soil, the placenta for the embryo of spring. "We should not despise the snowbanks," she said, "just as we should not fear pain or suffering or even tragedy. Maybe those are the womb in which we can be reborn into new life."

Door

One side of a door says "Push," the other says "Pull."

Push and pull are usually considered opposites. But there's no such thing as a door that you can only push, or only pull.

Conventional wisdom thinks of good and evil, right and wrong, sin and salvation, as opposites too. But maybe they're like two sides of a door.

Most of our sins, in fact, are virtues pushed to an extreme. Healthy self-esteem becomes arrogant pride; thrift becomes greed and avarice; the rituals of love become abuse, exploitation, or rape. Technology intended to enrich life pollutes the air and causes disease; medical science prolongs life past the point where life matters any more.

Like a door, all these things have two sides.

But the door of life isn't marked. It's up to us to know when to push forward, and when to pull back.

Chequebook

Many people treat their faith like a chequebook. By going to Sunday school, by going to church, by making regular charitable donations, they build up a bank account with God. When things go wrong, they expect to be able to write a cheque against that accumulation of good deeds.

But life doesn't work that way. We don't always get what we deserve. Bad things happen to good people – and good things can happen to bad people. The Reformation was launched, five centuries ago, on a simple premise: you can't buy your way into heaven' Grace is a gift from God, not a retirement savings plan.

Cheques themselves are worthless. They're just paper. If you wanted to, you could use them for grocery lists or telephone memos, and you'd be no worse off. Most of the time, cheques hide inside a purse, a pocket, or a briefcase – as invisible as their owner's faith.

A cheque becomes valuable only when you sign your name on it.

Which is, in a sense, what Jesus did with us. He signed his name on those who call themselves Christians, and made us valuable.

Shoes

An ancient tale tells of a country where everyone walked barefoot. Even the king had no covering for his feet. But in his castle, with polished marble floors covered with deep carpets, he didn't need anything to protect his tender tootsies.

One day, however, the king ventured outdoors. His feet encountered stones, twigs, and gravel. "Ooo! Ow! Ouch!" he cried. "This is terrible!"

Then, being a compassionate king, with the welfare of his subjects always at heart, he issued a decree: "No one should suffer this pain. Take cow hides, and lay the leather over all the land, to protect the people's feet from sticks and stones!"

Eventually, one of his advisors got enough nerve to suggest an alternative. "Sir, wouldn't it be easier just to cover the people's feet?"

And thus, says the ancient tale, were shoes invented.

Like that king, we sometimes want to change the entire world, to protect ourselves from pain of one kind or another. Sometimes we need to hear the advisor's alternative: the change might better take place in us.

Coffee mug

The optimist, according to a folk saying, thinks the coffee mug is half full; the pessimist thinks it's half empty. But both drink from their coffee mugs.

In our time, the coffee mug symbolizes socialization. Truck drivers and teenagers, gray-haired seniors and back-slapping sales reps, harried executives and unemployed transients – all gather over a mug of coffee and a doughnut. They do business; they renew friendships; they simply pass time together.

Churches serve coffee after their Sunday morning services, and there may be more genuine communion over that coffee than in the previous hour of formal worship.

If Jesus had lived in the 1990s, he would probably have raised a coffee mug, and said: "Each time you do this, remember me."

River

The river's clear water ran in a limpid chorus over rounded rocks.

It occurred to me, as I drove along beside the river, that I have never seen an ugly river. Every river, left to itself, is beautiful—whether it's a black canyon with raging waters or a muddy stream meandering across an ancient lake bottom.

Rivers only become ugly when we destroy them with warehouses and industries crowded along the banks, with toxins dumped into their waters, with debris carried by the current.

Every river is different. No two rivers ever follow the same watershed, the same valley. They all rise in their unique sources, and all follow their unique routes to the sea.

They're rather like us, that way. Each of our lives is unique. No two of us ever live exactly the same journey, the same experiences.

Yet, despite the uniqueness, we all flow to the same sea. The ancient Hebrews thought of the ocean as death, because it was too salty to drink or to use for irrigation. In a sense, the ocean is the death of every river.

Yet the ocean is not deadly. We now know it was the womb of life, the place where life began. It is still the world's most prolific source of living creatures.

There are many rivers, but only one ocean. We call the oceans by various names, but they are all connected. They are all at sea level.

If we are like rivers, perhaps the ocean is like God. Universal. Endless. The Alpha and the Omega, the beginning and the end. And perhaps, when we die, our individual rivers are all welcomed back into God's universal womb of life.